EVERYTHING I NEED TO KNOW
I LEARNED FROM

EVERYTHING I NEED TO KNOW
I LEARNED FROM
MISTER ROGERS' NEIGHBORHOOD®

Written by Melissa Wagner
Illustrations by Max Dalton

CLARKSON POTTER/PUBLISHERS

NEW YORK

CONTENTS

Introduction

SOME OF MY DEAREST CHILDHOOD MEMORIES
occurred in my grandmother's cozy living room.
Curled up on the floor in front of a 1970s-style console
television, watching *Mister Rogers' Neighborhood*,
I would observe my best adult friend change into
a sweater and sneakers, play music, and sing. He'd
introduce me to talented people, show me how
crayons and applesauce and wagons are made, and let

me peek into a colorful world where no one is perfect but everyone is accepted and appreciated. Then he'd tell me I was one of a kind and that people could like me just for being me.

Revisiting the shows as an adult, I realize there is a depth and intention behind *Mister Rogers' Neighborhood* that I didn't notice as a child. Hidden in plain sight are displays of some of my most deeply held beliefs and the messages I want to share with my daughter: You have value, and so does every other person, so treat yourself and others with care and respect. People's differences should be acknowledged and welcomed. It's okay to talk about the things that make us feel bad. Don't get so busy that you stop recognizing beauty and learning about the world.

In this book, you'll find quotes and anecdotes taken directly from television visits with Mister Rogers, his neighbors, and the familiar faces of the residents of the Neighborhood of Make-Believe. Mister Rogers was always focused on children, but his words are just as important and meaningful to adults.

<u>You Are Special</u>

"Everybody's special in
this life. Everybody you meet
has something special to give
and receive."

WE ARE ALL SPECIAL

Mister Rogers told each one of us that not only are
we special but also that each of our neighbors is
special, too. These core messages go hand in hand.
Each time he appeared on our television screens, his
love for people shone through. With each interaction
he had—whether with a child, a service worker,
a famous musician, or a familiar neighborhood
friend—he modeled appreciation for every person's
inherent worth.

"Everybody's different. And everybody's valuable. The world can be a better place because you were born into it."

VALUING OTHERS

Mister Rogers helped his neighbors recognize the goodness inside them. When Mr. McFeely arrived at Mister Rogers' house feeling sad after a delivery mishap, Mister Rogers listened as Mr. McFeely shared his feelings. Then he assured Mr. McFeely that everyone makes mistakes and reminded him of how grateful he was to have him in his life.

"Did you ever have anybody hurt your feelings? Did anyone ever say anything to you that made you feel really small and not very lovable? That feels awful, doesn't it? But isn't it nice when somebody helps you feel good about who you are? I mean, if you look for it, you'll probably find something fine inside of everybody."

"It's very important to look inside yourself and find that loving part of you. That's the part that you must take good care of and *never* be mean to. Because that's the part of you that allows you to love your neighbor. And your neighbor is anyone you happen to be with at any time in your life."

APPRECIATING THE WORK
THAT PEOPLE DO

Every one of us contributes something of value to the wider world. Whether in visits or on the Picture-Picture screen, Mister Rogers took us on tours of factories and workshops to show how people make the things we use every day. He explained each step of the process, peppering his commentary with compliments and admiring words—"This man surely works quickly and carefully, doesn't he?" and "She really knows her work"—that showed his respect for people and their efforts.

"I like to think of all the different things people make in this world. You know, even when it looks like complicated machinery is doing a lot of the work, it's important to remember that people made those machines. We wouldn't have any machines to do work if there hadn't been people to think them up and make them in the first place."

It's You
I Like

"You are a very special person.
There is only one just like you.
There's never been anyone
exactly like you in the history of
the earth, and there never will
be again. And people can like
you just because you're you."

YOU ARE LOVABLE

Before he left us for the day, Mister Rogers gave us the same kind of affirmation: "You make each day a special day by just being you." And through these feelings of appreciation and acceptance, we could grow and learn, feeling comfortable enough to allow ourselves to make mistakes and take risks. We could believe that we are valuable, and we are worthy, even when we fall short of our goals. "You don't have to do anything sensational for people to love you."

"It's such a good feeling to know that people can love us even when we're not perfect."

LADY ABERLIN: *I think you are just fine exactly the way you are.*

DANIEL: *The way I look?*

LADY ABERLIN: *Yes.*

DANIEL: *The way I talk?*

LADY ABERLIN: *Yes.*

DANIEL: *The way I love?*

LADY ABERLIN: *Especially that.*

DANIEL: *You don't think I'm a mistake?*

LADY ABERLIN: *You're the tiger I love most in this whole universe.*

DANIEL: *Oh thanks, Lady Aberlin. I love you, too.*

WHAT MATTERS MOST

Mister Rogers encouraged us to value our inner selves. When Henrietta Pussycat found out that Grandpère's beautiful granddaughter Collette would be visiting, Henrietta worried about her own place in the Neighborhood. She put on a fancy dress, a fancy hat, and makeup and would speak only French like Collette, even though her neighbors couldn't understand a word she said. Mister Rogers explained how she felt: "Henrietta thought that people wouldn't like her unless she got all dressed up in a fancy way. We've always liked Henrietta, no matter what she wore." He then sings "It's You I Like," reminding us that we, too, are loved for our essential selves rather than for our possessions and appearance.

"Our thoughts,
and our feelings,
the way we treat other
people, the way we
love one another—
that's what matters
much more than
what we look like."

"It's not so much what we have in this life that matters. It's what we do with what we have. The alphabet is fine, but it's what we do with it that matters most. Making words like 'friend' and 'love.' That's what really matters."

LOVING YOURSELF

Mister Rogers helped us appreciate our unique selves. When we feel comfortable with ourselves, we can talk about our feelings and make deeper connections with the people around us. Loving ourselves, and valuing what is special in us, can lead us to love and appreciate others.

"You can't love anybody else if you don't love yourself."

Lady Elaine Fairchilde

Be Generous with Your Gratitude

"Thank you. Two of the best words we can ever learn. In fact, 'thank you' is a way of saying 'I love you.'"

SHOWING YOUR APPRECIATION

Mister Rogers showed us the importance of gratitude and modeled ways for us to express it. We watched him write notes of appreciation and thank his guests for sharing their talents. When Mr. McFeely delivered a surprise gift to Mister Rogers—a marble sculpture from artist Allen Dwight—we saw Mister Rogers marveling at the art, examining it from all directions. "I like the way it feels," he said. "I like the way it looks; I like the way I feel when I'm looking at it. You know, the thing I think I like best about it is that you and Mr. Dwight thought to give it to me. Every time I look at it, I'll think of the two of you."

"When you make something for somebody, you hope that person will like it. Just as you hope that person likes you."

"Birthday presents and birthday parties are really little expressions of love. And it's feeling love that makes somebody feel good. That's the real present."

THE GIFT OF BEING A RECEIVER

Mister Rogers showed us that when we graciously accept a gift—or when we allow someone to help us, or when we express to someone how much we need them—we are giving others a good feeling in return. When Mister Rogers offered Mr. McFeely a couple of fortune cookies, Mr. McFeely gratefully accepted. After Mr. McFeely left, Mister Rogers closed the door behind him with a big smile on his face, saying, "Can you imagine why I'm feeling so happy right this minute? It has something to do with Mr. McFeely. It's because he was so pleased when I gave him the fortune cookies."

"It was like he was giving *me* a gift, the way he accepted mine."

ACCEPTING ALL GIFTS WITH GRACE

When King Friday XIII heard that Audrey Duck had written a poem that mentioned "queens and kings," he decided to celebrate Audrey's talent at a poetry reading in her honor. He ordered that all the neighbors be invited to hear her read. Audrey worried that her poem was too modest for such a big event, but the king insisted on proceeding. After a long introduction by him, Audrey read her short poem, and though the king was initially surprised that it wasn't more grandiose, he realized that even a modest gift is to be appreciated and he graciously thanked her: "It was the perfect length. It was a perfect poem. I found it just the proper length after my fine introduction. Applause again for our perfect poet, Audrey Duck."

"Being kind
is trying to think
what somebody
else might like,
and trying to help
them with it."

"Being kind has nothing
to do with your outsides.
No, kindness is an inside thing.
You can be very big outside, but
kind inside. You can be very
small outside, but very big
and kind inside."

Be a Helper

"Haven't you found that the best way to be happy is to be helping somebody else?"

MANY WAYS TO HELP

Time and again, in both his "real" neighborhood and in Make-Believe, Mister Rogers showed us how people could work together to help one another, with simple acts of kindness as well as larger gestures of care and support. We can all be helpers in all kinds of ways—big and small.

"What kinds of things are you good at helping with? I remember one child telling me one day, 'Mister Rogers, I'm only four years old, but I can do some kind things.' She was learning to be a helper. And I trust that you are, too."

"I'm proud of every good thing that you want to do for others."

HELPING IS LOVING

When King Friday discovered that the people in nearby Northwood had no food, he rallied his community to help. The neighbors sprang into action, planting gardens across the entire Neighborhood of Make-Believe to grow food to give to the residents of Northwood. Mister Rogers explained, "King Friday declared an all-out effort. You know what that means? It means that everyone will get out and make an effort to help. That kind of effort is a way of expressing love."

HEROES ARE EVERYDAY PEOPLE

In the Neighborhood of Make-Believe, we saw an example of neighbors offering support after a fire damaged the Platypus family home. Lady Aberlin, Handyman Negri, King Friday, and Lady Elaine formed a volunteer fire brigade to put out the fire. Lady Elaine offered her Museum-Go-Round as temporary shelter for the Platypus family, and the next day, Mayor Maggie and Neighbor Aber arrived from Westwood to bring supplies and help rebuild the Platypus Mound.

"When anybody's
in trouble, we try to
do what we can."

Neighbor Aber

NEIGHBORS HELPING NEIGHBORS

Mister Rogers introduced us to helpers all over his neighborhood. We met friendly teachers and crossing guards, artists and doctors, musicians and more. He showed us how people can contribute their own special skills and talents to make a neighborhood a better place to live.

"There are many helpful people in this world, aren't there? The more you grow into a helpful person yourself, the happier you'll find this world of ours is."

"When I was a boy and I would see scary things in the news, my mother would say to me, 'Look for the helpers. You will always find people who are helping.' To this day, especially in times of 'disaster,' I remember my mother's words and I am always comforted by realizing that there are still so many helpers— so many caring people in this world."

Feed the Fish

"It's fun to think about things like birds in the air, fish in the water, and animals and people walking on the earth. Yet all of us are alive, and we all need some kind of care."

"Everybody needs some kind of care."

BEING RESPONSIBLE

Mister Rogers' routine of feeding the fish in every episode showed us what it means to be a responsible caregiver. He helped us see the importance of being consistent in our care—in caring for others who rely on us, and in caring for ourselves. "The fish are not pretend. They are real, and they need care."

BEING A CAREGIVER

Mister Rogers knew that children want to feel useful
and needed just like adults do. Even though we were
children and there was a lot that we could not do
to help, there were some things that we could do.
He understood this innate desire, and he showed us
plenty of ways to take responsibility and care for our
family, friends, and pets. He also helped us recognize
our contributions, so we could feel proud of our
efforts. "Passing things at the table or getting your
mom's pocketbook or briefcase when she asks for it—
or giving someone a hug when you think they need
one. That's being a caregiver. You see, you're already a
caregiver, by many things that you do."

"The more you grow, the more care you can give. And the better you can feel about it."

"As you grow,
I trust that you are
finding many more ways
to show and tell
people that you love
them. Those are
the most important
things that you'll
ever learn to do."

*"Ugga mugga is just another way
of telling someone you love them."*

———

Lady Aberlin

TAKING CARE OF THE EARTH

Mister Rogers helped us develop an appreciation for the world around us. He introduced us to animals, showed us pictures of different kinds of fish, and urged us to look closely and carefully at plants and insects. He showed us how we could reuse throwaway items in our house, such as paper bags, cardboard boxes, and paper towel tubes. By fostering a love of nature and an awareness of how we can repurpose many of the things we already have, he encouraged us to grow into stewards of the earth.

"There is something fancy about every creature in our world. And there's something fine about each one of us, too. Each person, each fish, each animal, each bird. Each living creature. The important thing for us is to look for what's fine in everybody. And that will help us to want to take care of everybody."

All Kinds
of Feelings
Are Okay

"Everyone has lots of ways
of feeling. And all those ways
of feeling are fine. It's what
we do with our feelings that
matters in this life. I trust
that you are growing
in ways that will help you
with whatever feelings
you may have."

FEELINGS DON'T LAST FOREVER

Strong feelings can be scary—for children and for adults. We can be overwhelmed with emotion and feel unable to control our own responses. Mister Rogers regularly reminded us that all our feelings are natural, normal, and manageable. He talked about his own feelings as a child, and we knew he understood how children feel. He explained that though we may feel angry or sad for a while, we'd feel happy and glad again, too. And he gave us suggestions for how we could better manage our feelings.

"People's tears are like stars, because they're always there, but they just come out when people get sad or angry."

Daniel Striped Tiger

"Sometimes people are happy. Sometimes people are sad. Sometimes people are angry, and sometimes people are glad. What are you gonna do? That's just the way it is."

—————

Lady Elaine

TALKING ABOUT OUR FEELINGS

Mister Rogers encouraged us to talk about our feelings, especially with people we love and trust. When Prince Tuesday's parents left him at home with his day-and-night caregiver Neighbor Aber while they were out of town, the prince had lots of feelings about their trip. Prince Tuesday was eventually able to open up to Neighbor Aber about his worries and later to his parents. Ever the empathetic friend, Daniel Striped Tiger saw Prince Tuesday struggling and spoke with Mayor Maggie about how important it is to talk about feelings.

DANIEL: *Anything that people feel real strongly about is important to talk about.*

MAYOR MAGGIE: *Why do you think that is, Daniel?*

DANIEL: *I guess if you talk about something, it doesn't seem so scary.*

MAYOR MAGGIE: *Not so scary as when you sit and think about it all by yourself.*

DANIEL: *Yes. All-by-yourself times can be pretty scary.*

MAYOR MAGGIE: *Especially when there isn't somebody you love real close by.*

DANIEL: *But you can call and ask them to be with you.*

MAYOR MAGGIE: *Yes.*

DANIEL: *And sing to you. Mayor Maggie, will you sing to me?*

"There are many things we can do when we're feeling angry or sad or happy—many things that don't hurt ourselves or anybody else. Like exercises, or deep breathing, or music, or sports, or crafts— all sorts of things. In fact, they're some of the best things we can ever learn to do."

FINDING WAYS TO EXPRESS
OUR FEELINGS

Mister Rogers asked many of his special guests
how they expressed their feelings as musicians,
artists, or athletes. When cellist Yo-Yo Ma visited the
Neighborhood, he talked about how he could convey
his many moods through music. He demonstrated
how he might play when he felt happy, peaceful, or
angry, and shared that after he really dug in and used
his strength on an intense piece, he felt relieved.
"After having given all of this burst of energy, it felt
good," he said.

EVERYBODY FEELS MAD SOMETIMES

Lady Elaine was unable to control her anger when she grew frustrated with her inability to draw a picture of Grandpère's tower, so she used her magical Boomerang-Toomerang-Soomerang to turn it upside down. The neighbors urged her to return the tower to its upright position, but she refused. Eventually Lady Elaine's friend arrived with the ingredients for making play clay, and after they pounded the dough and talked about her feelings, Lady Elaine felt better enough to set the building right-side up again. Mister Rogers helped us know that there are many ways to manage our angry feelings.

"It really helps to talk about the way you feel. Because everyone has feelings, all the time."

You've Got to Do It

"I like to swim, but there
are some days I just don't feel
much like doing it. But I do it
anyway. I know it's good for me,
and I promised myself I'd do
it every day. And I like to keep
my promises. That's one of my
disciplines. . . . Inside you think,
I've kept at this, and I've really
learned it. Not by magic,
but by my own work."

TRYING YOUR BEST

We've all experienced the leap of faith required
to start a project or learn something new. It takes
courage to face a challenge and discipline to master
a new skill. When we were children, we had to take
risks to learn new things all the time. Mister Rogers
showed us that we couldn't just imagine something
into being—we'd have to *try* to make it happen. If we
wanted to learn to roller-skate, we weren't just going
to put on the skates and glide perfectly across the
floor. We needed to put in the effort to learn. We'd
fall, and we might even skin our knees, but once we
achieved our goal, we could take pride in it all the
more because of the work it took to master it.

"When I was young, I started to take clarinet lessons. But I just didn't practice, so I didn't learn. I think I wanted to learn by magic. I think I had the idea that if I got the clarinet, I would somehow know how to play it. It doesn't work that way. Magic doesn't work with learning. Not with anything really worthwhile."

"Did you hear how he said he has made lots of mistakes as he has learned new things? Everybody does. That's all part of trying. Of not being afraid of making mistakes. And as you keep trying, and you do better and better, it can give you such a good feeling."

IT'S OKAY TO MAKE MISTAKES

So many times, we imagine the perfect creation,
but when we try to reproduce our idea, the result is
nothing like the beautiful image in our mind. It can
stop us in our tracks. Mister Rogers reminded us that
it's usually impossible to learn new things *without*
making mistakes. We watched him laughing and
smiling as he awkwardly mixed up dance moves with
Ella Jenkins, dropped balls while juggling, and tried
to use a Hula-Hoop. He showed us by example that
we can have fun doing something even if we don't
do it just right.

PRACTICE!

Mister Rogers helped us know that practice and self-discipline are essential to accomplishing our goals. He often introduced us to musicians, dancers, artists, craftspeople, and athletes with extraordinary talents. Time and again, when talking to these guests, Mister Rogers asked them about how they started out and what it took for them to be able to do the things they do. He'd emphasize that even though their performances seem effortless, it actually took years of work and daily practice to reach their skill level. When professional tap dancer Sam Weber visited, Mister Rogers told us, "It may look easy when someone as good as Sam Weber does his dance and we're just looking at him. But it takes a lot of work to do dance really well. It's fun *and* it's a lot of work."

"When I was learning to play the piano, I made so many mistakes with the music, it didn't sound very good at all. . . . But my parents and my teacher told me that making mistakes was all part of learning. So I just kept at it, and I really enjoy it now."

"If there's something you really want to do, . . . it's worth all the practice time."

"The best way to learn something well is to ask somebody to help you with it. But it takes hours and hours of practice to be really good at it. In fact, it takes a lot of practice to be really good at almost everything. But it's worth it!"

ASKING FOR HELP

When we're experiencing the ups and downs of
learning a new skill, help from someone who cares
can make all the difference. When Prince Tuesday got
a new bicycle from his parents, he grew frustrated
with learning how to ride. Handyman Negri happened
upon the prince, who told him that he'd been
practicing for a whole day, but the bicycle wouldn't
stay up long enough for him to ride it. Handyman
Negri explained that learning often takes much longer
than one day, and he offered to help. Later, with
Handyman Negri's continued support, Prince Tuesday
told Ana Platypus that he felt like throwing his bike
away because he was so angry but that having the
help of Handyman Negri made him feel better. What a
nice reminder of how a good teacher can empower us
to feel so much better about ourselves as we learn.

Don't Forget the Fun

"Do you ever feel as if you just have to play? That's an important feeling. . . . It helps you know who you are and who you want to be. . . . No matter what game you play, you can be yourself, and that's all you ever have to be."

PLAYING IS LEARNING

Mister Rogers took play seriously, and he let us know how essential it is for growing all through our lives. As he played, he showed us that play could help us try on new roles and master new skills and learn about the world, no matter how old we are.

"Playing is one of the most important things you can do when you're a child. And if you're learning to make up your own kind of play with whatever plaything you have, you're learning one of the most important things for growing."

USING YOUR IMAGINATION

Mister Rogers encouraged children to play and explore. With him, we imagined stories about the Neighborhood of Make-Believe, where anything can happen—a boomerang can turn the world upside down, Purple Panda can magically appear and disappear, and cereal can fall like snow. In his television house, we could pretend an empty cardboard box was almost anything!

"Did you ever grow anything
in a vegetable garden?
Or a flower garden?
Do you ever grow anything
in the garden of your mind?
Sure. You can grow ideas
in your mind. You can think
about things and make
believe things, and that's
like growing something
of your own. You have
wonderful ideas. All you
have to do is think about
them and they'll grow."

"Playing can help your feelings, too. Many children I know seem to be able to play about their worries, and sometimes feel some comfort for their sadness."

PLAY IS IMPORTANT

When Bob Dog became hurt while he was playing, King Friday made a rule banning all play in the Neighborhood. He thought it was a way to keep everyone safe. But Lady Elaine didn't want to live in a place where there was no play allowed, so she used her Boomerang-Toomerang-Soomerang to magically move her Museum-Go-Round to a park where she was free to play. Everyone was sad, so they decided to go against the king's ruling and built a new playground of their own. The king was upset when he saw it, and it was Prince Tuesday, the king's son, who stood up to his father. He explained that everyone needs to play. He helped his father realize he was wrong, and the king reversed his rule. Mister Rogers helped us realize that big or small, all of us need to play as a way to express ourselves.

"Some of the things that you feel like doing to express yourself when you're little you keep developing all during your lifetime. That's one of the great things about people growing."

YOU CAN PLAY AT ANY AGE

Mister Rogers showed us how adults can be playful, too. We saw him roller-skating at a roller rink and playing mini golf with Mr. McFeely. We also saw how music presents an opportunity for play, as when Mister Rogers laughingly sat at a child-size toy piano, joining Joe Negri on guitar and Bob Rawsthorne on stump fiddle for a whimsical *Concerto for Toys*. Their smiles and laughter made it clear what a great time they were having.

"Did you ever try your shoes on your hands? It's fun to think of different things like that, isn't it? It's like playing with ideas. In fact, that's how people invent new things. They just start to play with ideas and let their imaginations have a good time."

When You're Wondering, You're Learning

"I spend a lot of time trying to learn about things. I'm curious. And I wonder about all sorts of things.... We learn so much by wondering."

NOTICING EVERYDAY BEAUTY

Mister Rogers shared his enthusiasm and appreciation for the world with us. He nurtured our curiosity by encouraging us to closely examine the things he brought to share with us, be it a bottle of bubbles, a colorful handmade quilt, or an intricate model airplane. He invited us to join him in admiring new things every day. When he snorkled with oceanographer Sylvia Earle in a coral reef, we witnessed his reverence for the beauty of the ocean and all its wildlife.

"Wondering
and
marveling
is never a
waste
of time."

"We have so many things that we think about and feel and are curious about, don't we? Of course! That's how we learn things. We think about them, we have feelings about them, we're curious about them—that's part of who we are."

"Being curious
about things
really helps us
to learn."

"I like to learn new things. And learning more and more about old things. I've always wanted to know how things work, and how people make things work."

STAYING CURIOUS

Mister Rogers introduced us to so many talented people—musicians and artists, athletes and dancers— and invited us to watch them do what they loved. As he observed them, he asked questions that demonstrated his curiosity and helped us appreciate talented people, too. He reacted with open appreciation for their efforts, whether it was a ballet dancer unfolding her body like a flower, a child break-dancing, or a juggler keeping several balls in the air at once.

"It makes me feel good to see people who are doing something they love to do and enjoying the work of it. Isn't it wonderful to think that each one of us has a different talent, something that we can use to help us and somebody else?"

SLOWING DOWN

One way that Mister Rogers encouraged us to marvel was by giving us plenty of time to contemplate and examine the things he brought to share with us each visit. He might hold up a toy and turn it over in his hand, inviting us to look at it from all angles, showing us how it worked several times while asking questions to stimulate our curiosity. He let us focus and observe, sometimes in total silence. He once asked us to examine an African violet for a full twenty-five seconds, encouraging us to "take a long look." When we were through, he asked, "Do you like to look at something like this plant really carefully? If you do, that's one way to know you're growing."

"Every once
in a while, do you
just like to take
your time with what
you're doing?"

We Are All Neighbors

"Everybody's different.
And there are some things
about everybody that are
the same. That's what's
wonderful. That's what helps
us to understand each other.
That we've got some things
inside of us that are the same
as somebody else's.
We're all human beings."

WE'RE EACH UNIQUE, YET WE'RE ALL THE SAME

Mister Rogers was welcoming to all visitors. Through him, we met people from different cultural and racial backgrounds with a range of abilities, skills, and strengths. We watched Mister Rogers approach every person with delight, and we understood his appreciation for each visitor—the qualities and experiences that made their particular visit something new and exciting to celebrate.

"We can always try to remember that we're much more than one thing. We're much more than our arms or our legs or our eyes or our skin or our hair. We're even more than our thoughts."

"Once you get
to know people,
you find that there
is much more to
them than what you
see when you look
at their 'outsides.'
It's the heart and
not just the eyes
that discovers what's
real about us."

DANIEL: *Mr. Clemmons, why is everybody so different on the outside and so similar on the inside?*

FRANÇOIS CLEMMONS: *I don't know. We do look very different, but we have many of the same feelings.*

DANIEL: *I get sad sometimes. Do you?*

FRANÇOIS CLEMMONS: *Of course I do.*

DANIEL: *And I get really happy sometimes. Do you?*

FRANÇOIS CLEMMONS: *I certainly do. And you know one of the reasons I'm happy right now?*

DANIEL: *Why?*

FRANÇOIS CLEMMONS: *Because I enjoy talking about serious things with you.*

"Each one of us is special, and it's because of who we are inside. You and your family and your neighbors—we're all different, and we all have something to offer our world. And I trust that you're growing to understand that well."

"Everybody's different. And everybody's valuable."

"Every time you look at somebody, please remember that nobody else in the whole world is exactly like that person. That person is one of a kind. Just like you. Isn't that wonderful?"

ABOUT THE AUTHORS

FRED ROGERS PRODUCTIONS
inspires a lifetime of learning by
creating quality children's media that
models an enthusiasm for learning
and earns the trust of parents and
caregivers.

MELISSA WAGNER is a writer and
editor who had the honor of working
with Fred Rogers on several books,
including *The Mister Rogers Parenting
Book* and *Mister Rogers' Playtime*. She
lives in Pittsburgh with her husband
and their daughter.

MAX DALTON is a graphic artist and
illustrator whose work is featured in
The Wes Anderson Collection. He lives in
Buenos Aires, Argentina.

"Neighborhood Trolley" and characters from *Mister Rogers'
Neighborhood*™ by McFeely-Rogers Foundation. Used with
permission.

Published in the United States by Clarkson Potter/Publishers,
an imprint of Random House, a division of
Penguin Random House LLC, New York.
clarksonpotter.com

CLARKSON POTTER is a trademark and POTTER with colophon
is a registered trademark of Penguin Random House LLC.

Library of Congress Cataloging-in-Publication Data is available
upon request.

ISBN 978-1-9848-2644-2
Ebook ISBN 978-1-9848-2645-9

Printed in China

Cover and interior design by Danielle Deschenes
Cover illustration by Danielle Deschenes
Interior illustrations by Max Dalton

10 9 8 7 6 5 4 3 2 1

First Edition

Fred
Rogers
PRODUCTIONS